"FINALLY COMES A GREAT, PRACTICAL BOOK FOR PREPARING YOUTH FINANCIALLY! IT HAS BEEN A DECADE SINCE A GOOD PREPARATORY BOOK HAS BEEN AVAILABLE FOR KIDS ON THIS SUBJECT. STANLEY STEPPES HAS PREPARED AN INSIGHTFUL ENGAGING BOOK FOR YOUTH AND HERE'S A SECRET:... ITS A GREAT RESOURCE FOR PARENTS TO BONE UP ON HOW TO TALK WITH THEIR KIDS TOO! A SMART AUTHOR HAS WRITTEN AN INSPIRING BOOK FOR MAKING KIDS SMART ABOUT FINANCIAL EDUCATION. A WINNING FORMULA FOR ANY FAMILY IN THESE ECONOMIC TIMES. BRAVO!"

DR. SCOTT PREISSLER, PH.D., M.S., M.ED.
EDKLUND PROFESSOR OF STEWARD LEADERSHIP
SCHOOL OF THEOLOGY
SOUTHWESTERN BAPTIST THEOLOGICAL SEMINARY

REVIEWS

"MONEY SMART KIDS: CHRISTIAN AND DADDY GO SHOPPING IS A GREAT WAY TO BEGIN TEACHING YOUR CHILDREN ABOUT MONEY EARLY. STANLEY HAS TAKEN A COMPLICATED TOPIC EVEN FOR ADULTS AND MADE IT FUN AND INTERESTING FOR KIDS!"

DORETHIA R. CONNER, MBA, FINANCIAL EXPERT

"IF YOU WANT TO GIVE YOUR CHILDREN OR GRANDCHILDREN A HEAD START IN LIFE, I WOULD SERIOUSLY READ THEM 'CHRISTIAN AND DADDY GO SHOPPING.' TEACHING YOUR CHILDREN ABOUT MONEY FROM AN EARLY AGE CREATES A STRONG FOUNDATION FOR THEIR FUTURE."

LOUIS BARAJAS, AUTHOR OF MY STREET MONEY
A STREET LEVEL VIEW OF MANAGING YOUR MONEY FROM THE HEART TO THE BANK

"THUMBS UP TO STANLEY FOR RECOGNIZING THE NEED FOR FINANCIAL LITERACY SHOULD BEGIN AS EARLY AS POSSIBLE. BY IMPLEMENTING HIS IDEAS WITH YOUNG CHILDREN HE IS ABLE TO FOSTER A MINDSET THAT HOPEFULLY MAKES THE RESPONSIBILITY OF FINANCIAL MANAGEMENT LESS DAUNTING LATER IN THEIR LIVES."

GREG KELSER SPORTS COMMENTATOR AND MOTIVATIONAL SPEAKER

"THIS BOOK SHOULD BE ON THE BOOKSHELF OF EVERY CHILD RIGHT NEXT TO CHARLIE BROWN! IT OFFERS GOOD READING WITH A REAL LIFE APPLICATION."

SHEILA DORSEY, ASSISTANT SUPERINTENDENT
KALAMAZOO PUBLIC SCHOOLS

MONEY SMART KIDS

PRESENTS

CHRISTIAN & DADDY GO SHOPPING

STORY BY STANLEY M. STEPPES,
BROUGHT TO LIFE BY KENJJI,
EDITED BY SONYA BERNARD-HOLLINS

CHRISTIAN AND DADDY GO SHOPPING

STORY BY STANLEY M. STEPPES, BROUGHT TO LIFE BY KENJJI
EDITED BY SONYA BERNARD-HOLLINS

EVERY TIME CHRISTIAN CAME INTO THE STORE
HE WAS AMAZED BY ALL THE ITEMS ON THE SHELVES.
HE SAW SHIRTS, SHOES, EVEN A RED FIRE TRUCK.
HE RAN TOWARD IT AND JUST AS HE WAS ABOUT
TO ASK DADDY IF HE COULD HAVE IT, DADDY SAID,
"TODAY WE ARE SHOPPING FOR MOMMY." CHRISTIAN
SMILED REMEMBERING HIS JOB FOR THE DAY.

CHRISTIAN WANTED TO MAKE MOMMY HAPPY, SO HE BEGAN POINTING TO THE PERFUME, EARRINGS, AND ALL THE BEAUTIFUL THINGS HE KNEW HIS MOMMY WOULD LOVE.

"CHRISTIAN, WE DON'T HAVE ENOUGH MONEY FOR ALL OF THOSE THINGS," SAID DADDY.

"WHY DON'T WE HAVE ENOUGH MONEY FOR EVERYTHING?"

"YOU HAVE A LOT OF MONEY IN YOUR WALLET. HUNDREDS OF MONEY," CHRISTIAN EXCLAIMED.

DADDY REALIZED THAT HE HADNT TALKED WITH HIS SON ABOUT THE IMPORTANCE OF MONEY AND WHAT IT WAS USED FOR. HE TOOK CHRISTIAN BY THE HAND AND LED HIM TO A QUIET TABLE AT THE FOOD COURT. HE NEEDED TO EXPLAIN THE RESPONSIBILITY OF SPENDING BEFORE THEY WENT ANY FURTHER.

LESSON 1:
WHAT IS MONEY?

MONEY HELPS DADDY AND MOMMY TAKE CARE OF YOU.

"CHRISTIAN, WE HAVE A HOME, CAR, AND YOU HAVE YOUR OWN ROOM WITH CLOTHES IN YOUR CLOSET AND PLENTY OF TOYS."

"WE HAVE FOOD TO EAT, LIGHTS TO SEE, AND HEAT TO KEEP US WARM. MOST OF THE THINGS WE PROVIDE FOR YOU AND YOUR BROTHER COST MONEY."

DADDY PULLED COINS FROM HIS POCKET.

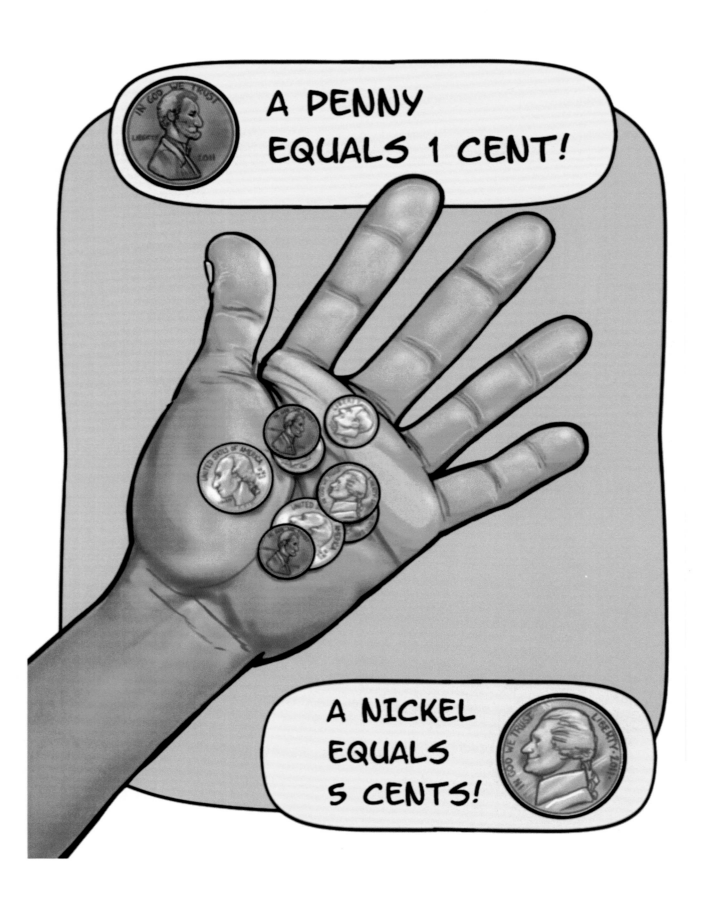

A DIME EQUALS 10 CENTS!

A QUARTER EQUALS 25 CENTS!

DADDY PULLED OUT HIS SMARTPHONE TO SHOW CHRISTIAN A PICTURE OF THE HALF DOLLAR AND GOLDEN COINS.

A HALF DOLLAR EQUALS 50 CENT!

A DOLLAR COIN EQUALS $1.00

CHRISTIAN JINGLED THE COINS IN HIS HANDS AND SPREAD OUT THE DOLLARS ONTO THE TABLE NICE AND NEAT. HE WAS VERY INTERESTED IN THE COINS AND LOOKED THEM OVER CAREFULLY.

HE POINTED AT THE QUARTER IN HIS DADDY'S HAND AND ASKED HOW MANY TOYS THEY COULD BUY WITH IT.

YOU SEE THAT MACHINE OVER THERE? IT SAYS 25 CENTS. I'M AFRAID THAT'S ALL THE TOY YOU CAN GET FOR A QUARTER," DADDY LAUGHED.
CHRISTIAN DIDN'T FIND IT TOO FUNNY, BUT CONTINUED TO LISTEN TO DADDY.

THIS BILL IS WORTH ONE DOLLAR...

...AND EQUALS 100 PENNIES OR FOUR QUARTERS.

THIS BILL IS WORTH FIVE DOLLARS AND IS EQUAL TO 5 ONE DOLLAR BILLS.

THIS BILL IS WORTH TEN DOLLARS AND
IS EQUAL TO 2 FIVE DOLLAR BILLS.

CHRISTIAN'S EYES WERE WIDE OPEN AND
HE LOOKED AT HIS DADDY AND SAID
"WE ARE RICH!"

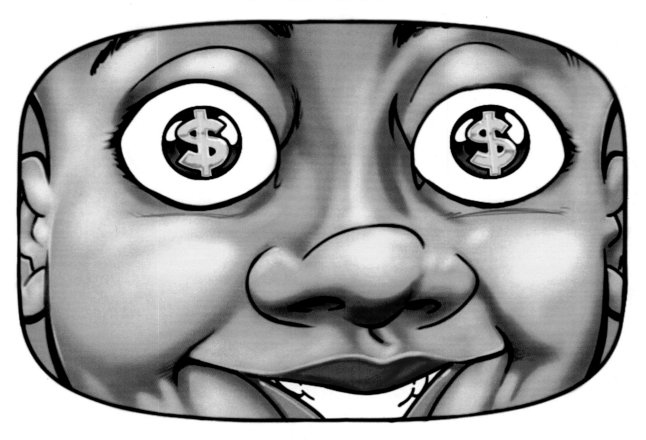

DADDY EXPLAINED TO HIS SON THAT SEEING A LOT OF
MONEY IN SOMEONES HAND DOES NOT MEAN THEY ARE
RICH. HE TOLD CHRISTIAN THAT MOMMY AND DADDY
HAVE ENOUGH MONEY TO PAY FOR EVERYTHING THEY
NEED LIKE THEIR HOME, FOOD, CLOTHES, AND SOME OF
THE THINGS THEY WANT LIKE AN IPAD OR A FAMILY
VACATION. SO THAT MEANS WE CANNOT BUY
EVERYTHING WE SEE ON TELEVISION.

CHRISTIAN DIDN'T LIKE HEARING THEY COULD NOT BUY EVERYTHING THEY WANTED, BUT HIS DAD REMINDED HIM THAT THEY DID HAVE ENOUGH MONEY TO BUY MOMMY SOMETHING REALLY NICE FOR HER BIRTHDAY. CHRISTIAN PERKED UP AGAIN AND ASKED HIS DADDY TO SHOW HIM THE LAST BILLS REMAINING IN DADDY'S WALLET.

DADDY TOLD CHRISTIAN THAT EVERY AMOUNT OF MONEY
CAN BE MADE BY USING OTHER AMOUNTS OF MONEY.

 FOR EXAMPLE, "YOU CAN MAKE ONE DOLLAR..."

"...BY ADDING FOUR QUARTERS."

DADDY PULLED A BILL FROM HIS POCKET.

"THIS BILL IS WORTH ONE HUNDRED DOLLARS..."

"...AND EQUALS 10 TEN DOLLAR BILLS."

"DADDY, YOU SAID ADD. I KNOW WHAT ADD MEANS," CHRISTIAN SAID WITH EXCITEMENT. "MY TEACHER MRS. JOHNSON SAYS THAT IS MATH."
"THAT'S RIGHT CHRISTIAN; IF YOU WANT TO BE GOOD WITH MONEY YOU MUST ALSO UNDERSTAND MATH." SAID DADDY.

LESSON 2:
SPENDING PLANS

"YOU KNOW WHAT A PIE LOOKS LIKE?" DADDY ASKED.
"OH YES, YUMMY CHERRY PIE," CHRISTIAN SAID LICKING HIS LIPS.
"WELL, EACH SLICE OF THE MONEY PIE IS MEANT FOR SOMETHING
DIFFERENT THAT WE NEED TO PURCHASE."

"IT IS VERY IMPORTANT TO REMEMBER THAT
THERE IS ONLY SO MUCH PIE THAT IS AVAILABLE.
ONCE IT IS GONE IT IS GONE, AT LEAST UNTIL WE MAKE
A NEW PIE. CHRISTIAN CHUCKLED."

"WE SHOULD MAKE A LIST OF WHAT WE NEED AND THE COST SO WE SPEND THE CORRECT AMOUNTS, RIGHT DADDY?"

"THAT IS A GREAT IDEA SON. YOU ARE BECOMING MONEY SMART." DADDY GRABBED HIS CALCULATOR FROM HIS JACKET POCKET. "THE AMOUNT ON THE SCREEN IS ONE HUNDRED SIXTY SIX DOLLARS AND FORTY ONE CENTS."

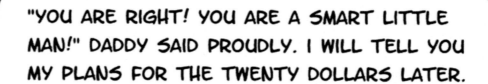

"DADDY, THAT'S NOT THE SAME MONEY YOU HAVE IN YOUR WALLET," CHRISTIAN SAID WISELY.

"YOU ARE RIGHT! YOU ARE A SMART LITTLE MAN!" DADDY SAID PROUDLY. I WILL TELL YOU MY PLANS FOR THE TWENTY DOLLARS LATER.

LESSON 3:
MAKING SPENDING DECISIONS

"SINCE WE ARE HAVING A TOUGH TIME FINDING A SCARF, LET'S LOOK AT THE GLOVES AND SEE IF ANY ARE WITHIN OUR BUDGET." DADDY AND CHRISTIAN SAW PLENTY OF GLOVES BUT THEY WERE ALL ABOVE TEN DOLLARS. CHRISTIAN WAS UPSET AGAIN BECAUSE HE REALLY WANTED TO GET MOMMY A SCARF AND GLOVES TO GO WITH HER SWEATER.

"I HAVE AN IDEA. LET'S LOOK AT THE SWEATERS AGAIN AND SEE IF WE CAN FIND A REALLY NICE ONE FOR LESS MONEY. IF WE DO THAT WE COULD STILL BUY MOMMY A SCARF AND GLOVES.

DADDY AND CHRISTIAN ARRIVED AT THE CHECKOUT LINE WITH THEIR BASKET. THE WOMAN AT THE REGISTER SMILED AT CHRISTIAN WHO WAS SO EXCITED THAT HE TOLD HER THEY HAD PURCHASED SOME GIFTS FOR HIS MOMMY'S BIRTHDAY. DADDY ALLOWED CHRISTIAN TO HAND THE MONEY TO THE CASHIER TO PAY FOR THE ITEMS. THE CASHIER HANDED CHRISTIAN A RECEIPT AND THEY WALKED OUT OF THE STORE.

THAT EVENING DADDY WALKED INTO CHRISTIAN'S BEDROOM AND TOLD HIM THAT HE WAS PROUD OF HIM. HE ASKED CHRISTIAN IF HE REMEMBERED THAT THEY DIDN'T SPEND ALL THE MONEY THAT DADDY HAD WITH HIM. CHRISTIAN NODDED HIS HEAD AND SAID, "I REMEMBER." DADDY PULLED A GIFT FROM BEHIND HIS BACK.

"THIS IS FOR YOU, FOR DOING SUCH A GOOD JOB AT THE STORE HELPING TO BUY SOMETHING NICE FOR MOMMYS BIRTHDAY."

DADDY HANDED HIM A CRISP $20 BILL FOR HIS PENNY BANK.

CHRISTIAN WAS ELATED. "I'LL SAVE THIS, DADDY, UNTIL I FIND SOMETHING IN MY BUDGET TO BUY," HE SMILED. DADDY KISSED HIM GOODNIGHT.

THE END

I THANK MY WONDERFUL WIFE ABRA,
AND OUR BOYS, CHRISTIAN AND CARTER FOR SUPPORTING
ME IN THIS PROJECT.

CHRISTIAN, YOU ARE TRULY ONE OF THE HEROES IN MY LIFE.
YOU ARE ONE OF THE GREATEST GIFTS IN MY LIFE AND HAVE
TAUGHT ME MORE ABOUT FAITH, LOVE, AND HOPE THROUGH
FATHERHOOD THAN I COULD EVER TEACH YOU ABOUT MONEY.

THANK YOU TO ALL THE TALENTED PEOPLE WHO HELPED
WITH THIS BOOK AND THE MONEY SMART KIDS BRAND,
ESPECIALLY KENJJI, SONYA BERNARD-HOLLINS, AND THE
MANY OTHER FAMILY AND FRIENDS THAT HAVE GIVEN
THEIR SUPPORT.

ABOUT THE AUTHOR

STANLEY M. STEPPES IS A WEALTH ADVISOR, FINANCIAL EDUCATOR, SPEAKER, AND WRITER. HE SERVES AS THE PRESIDENT & DIRECTOR OF ADVISORY SERVICES OF CHRISTIAN ALEXANDER WEALTH ADVISORS, LLC, AN INDEPENDENTLY OWNED COMPREHENSIVE WEALTH ADVISORY PRACTICE SERVING INDIVIDUALS AND FAMILIES AT EACH STAGE IN LIFE.

HE IS A QUALIFIED FINANCIAL PROFESSIONAL COMPLETING THE SERIES7, 63 AND 65 LICENSING EXAMS AND STATE OF MICHIGAN LIFE & VARIABLE ANNUITY REQUIREMENTS. HE BEGAN HIS CAREER IN THE FINANCIAL SERVICES SECTOR AT THE AGE OF 16, WORKING FOR SEVERAL ORGANIZATIONS SINCE AS A FINANCIAL CONSULTANT AND REGISTERED FINANCIAL ADVISOR. HE STARTED CHRISTIAN ALEXANDER WEALTH ADVISORS, LLC IN 2009.

IN ADDITION, STANLEY IS THE FOUNDER & CEO OF FINANCIAL LITERACY PARTNERS OF AMERICA, L3C, A MICHIGAN LOW-PROFIT LIMITED LIABILITY COMPANY PROVIDING FINANCIAL LITERACY EDUCATION, COACHING, AND TRAINING TO FOR-PROFIT AND NON-PROFIT ORGANIZATIONS THROUGH WORKSHOPS AND SEMINARS.

STANLEY HAS DEDICATED HIS LIFE TO PROVIDE INDIVIDUALS AND FAMILIES WITH THE INFORMATION AND GUIDANCE THEY NEED TO BECOME FINANCIALLY FREE.

HE RESIDES IN KALAMAZOO, MICHIGAN WITH HIS LOVELY WIFE ABRA, AN 8TH GRADE ENGLISH TEACHER AND THEIR TWO BOYS, CHRISTIAN AND CARTER.

ABOUT THE ARTIST

KENJJI IS AN AWARD WINNING ARTIST THAT HAS CREATED COMICS AND CARICATURES INDEPENDENTLY FOR OVER 20 YEARS. KENJJI'S ILLUSTRATIONS HAVE APPEARED IN THE NEW YORK TIMES, ORLANDO, WIRED MAGAZINE AND MORE. AS A FREELANCE ARTIST KENJJI HAS A CLIENT LIST INCLUDING MTV, ABSOLUT VODKA, THE DETROIT LIONS, AND MICHIGAN FIRST NATIONAL BANK.

BEYOND HIS PUBLISHED WORK KENJJI ENJOYS DRAWING LIVE FOR VARIOUS AUDIENCES. KENJJI HAS TAUGHT CARTOONING CLASSES FOR THE YMCA, THE COLLEGE FOR CREATIVE STUDIES, AND THE KALAMAZOO PUBLIC LIBRARY. KENJJI ALSO DRAWS CARICATURES FOR VARIOUS EVENTS AND PRIVATE PARTIES MOST RECENTLY DRAWING LIVE AT THE DETROIT AUTO SHOW WHICH BOASTED 750,000 IN ATTENDANCE.

KENJJI MAY BE AVAILABLE FOR YOUR ARTISTIC NEEDS SEE MORE OF HIS WORK ONLINE AT KENJJI.COM

ABOUT THE EDITOR

SONYA BERNARD-HOLLINS IS AN AWARD-WINNING WRITER WHO HAS EARNED AWARDS FROM THE MICHIGAN PRESS ASSOCIATION, THE ASSOCIATED PRESS OF MICHIGAN, GANNETT, AND OTHERS. SHE HAS WORKED AS A JOURNALIST AND FREELANCE CONTRIBUTOR TO BLACK ENTERPRISE MAGAZINE, AND VARIOUS MAGAZINES AND MIDWEST NEWSPAPERS.

SONYA HAS BEEN RECOGNIZED FOR HER COMMUNITY SERVICE BY SUCH ORGANIZATIONS AS THE A. PHILIP RANDOLPH ASSOCIATION (BATTLE CREEK CHAPTER), AMERICAN BUSINESS WOMENS ASSOCIATION (BATTLE CREEK CHAPTER), WESTERN MICHIGAN UNIVERSITY, KALAMAZOO VALLEY COMMUNITY COLLEGE, AND HERITAGE BATTLE CREEK.

THE WESTERN MICHIGAN UNIVERSITY GRADUATE HAS TAKEN HER PASSION FOR EDUCATING YOUNG GIRLS THROUGH TRAVEL AND MEDIA, TO FORM THE MERZE TATE TRAVEL CLUB, WHICH HAS BEEN FEATURED ON NATIONAL PUBLIC RADIO WITH KYLE NORRIS, THE MICHAEL ERIC DYSON SHOW IN BALTIMORE, MARYLAND, WMUK WITH GORDON EVANS, AND 1560 AM THE TOUCH WITH HOST BUDDY HANNAH.

SONYA IS THE AUTHOR OF THE BOOK, "HERE I STAND: A MUSICAL HISTORY OF AFRICAN AMERICANS IN BATTLE CREEK, MICHIGAN," AND PUBLISHER OF COMMUNITY VOICES MAGAZINE. SHE LIVES IN KALAMAZOO, MICH. WITH HER HUSBAND, SEAN, AND THEIR FOUR CHILDREN.

IMPORTANT TERMS

AFFORD: TO BE ABLE TO PAY FOR.

BUDGET: A STATEMENT OF ESTIMATED INCOME AND EXPENSES. A PLAN FOR USING MONEY

BUY: TO ACQUIRE POSSESSION, OWNERSHIP, OR RIGHTS TO THE USE OR SERVICES OF BY PAYMENT ESPECIALLY OF MONEY.

COST: THE AMOUNT PAID OR CHARGED FOR SOMETHING.

CURRENCY: MONEY IN CIRCULATION (AS COINS, TREASURY NOTES, AND BANKNOTES): A MEDIUM OF EXCHANGE: COMMON USE OR ACCEPTANCE.

EXCHANGE: THE ACT OF GIVING OR TAKING ONE THING IN RETURN FOR ANOTHER.

MATH (MATHEMATICS): THE SCIENCE THAT IS CONCERNED WITH NUMBERS AND THEIR PROPERTIES, RELATIONS, AND OPERATIONS AND WITH SHAPES IN SPACE AND THEIR STRUCTURE AND MEASUREMENT.

IMPORTANT TERMS

MONEY: SOMETHING (SUCH AS COINS OR BILLS) GENERALLY ACCEPTED AS A WAY OF MEASURING VALUE, AS A WAY TO TRADE VALUE, AND AS A WAY TO PAY FOR GOODS AND SERVICES.

NEED: SOMETHING NECESSARY OR DESIRED: A MENTAL OR PHYSICAL REQUIREMENT FOR KEEPING A LIVING THING IN NORMAL CONDITION.

RICH: HAVING GREAT WEALTH: HAVING A LARGE SUPPLY OF SOME USUALLY DESIRABLE QUALITY OR THING.

SALES TAX: A TAX BASED ON THE COST OF THE ITEM(S) PURCHASED AND COLLECTED DIRECTLY FROM THE BUYER.

SPENDING: TO PAY OUT.

WANT: TO DESIRE, WISH, OR LONG FOR SOMETHING.

TERMS ADAPTED FROM DICTIONARY.COM

19314080R00027

Made in the USA
Middletown, DE
13 April 2015